SERMON OUTLINES

on

The Inner Life

T0311324

Charles R. Wood

PUBLICATIONS

Grand Rapids, MI 49501

Sermon Outlines on the Inner Life

Copyright © 2006 by Charles R. Wood

Published in 2006 by Kregel Publications, a division of Kregel, Inc., P.O. Box 2607, Grand Rapids, MI 49501.

ISBN 978-0-8254-4153-0

Printed in the United States of America

3 4 5 6 / 13 12

Contents

Introduction

In the present moment the life of the church is experiencing a growing dissatisfaction with the externalism that has marked so much believing Christianity for the past half century. Men and women, and especially young men and women, are no longer content to have their spirituality either defined by or judged by the things they wear, the places they go, and the things they do. They are looking for something deeper, something more real and lasting.

The "deeper life" teaching of a past generation is too subjective and esoteric to appeal to this pragmatic generation, so something else is necessary if the longings of many hearts are to find fulfillment in Christianity and the local church. A modern generation is often criticized by an older generation for its shallow approach to Christian music and worship. Regardless of the accuracy of such accusations, it is increasingly evident that this generation cannot accurately be accused of lacking a desire for depth in its commitment to its faith.

The sermons included in this volume deal with the realities of the inner person and its relationship to the Word of God and the God of the Word. These sermons, however, are not subjective and ethereal. They are based on a careful study of the meaning of Scripture and its relationship to the real world in which the average Christian lives, and they are designed for practical application to life "where the rubber meets the road."

Although the compiler of these sermons is of the older generation, his heart and mind are solidly grounded in the present. The sermons are "in touch" in the truest sense as the crucible of experience has granted insight into the fallacy of both externalism and subjectivism when it comes to defining the Christian life. The congregation to which these sermons were preached was relatively youthful but one that included the whole gamut of social and economic classes.

As is always true of sermon outlines of this nature, they are designed to be preached after some period of personal preparation. There is no shortcut to effective preaching. The use of another's outline is merely a starting point in one's preparation. Careful reading of the indicated Scripture (and its context); consultation with one or more commentaries; and careful, prayerful consideration will provide background more conducive to the type of preaching that genuinely reaches the inner person.

Modern Christians may appear superficial and shallow; it has been my experience that their hearts are neither. Solid preaching on the internal aspects of biblical truth and a consistent emphasis on the importance of reality will never be without fruit. Whatever the importance attached to externals, they will never be of genuine spiritual value unless they arise out of internal commitments. It is the prayer of the compiler that these sermons may be used of God to drive modern Christians deeper into a relationship with Him that is genuine and satisfying.

CHARLES R. WOOD

Filled with His Own Ways

Proverbs 14:14

Introduction:

"The backslider in heart shall be filled with his own ways." This is nowhere more evident than in the life of Lot. Lot is one of the saddest characters in the Bible, and his life screams a warning to us: "Don't end up filled with your own ways!"

I. **The Steps of His Backsliding**
    A. A wrong choice (Gen. 13:11)
        1. Remember—the choice here is really a small thing
        2. It was just one in a series of choices in his life
    B. A wrong move (Gen. 13:12)
        1. It was not a huge move; they lived in the area anyway
        2. It was more a change of direction than a move
    C. A wrong location (Gen. 14:12)
        1. It was just another small step
        2. The move put him right in the heart of what he had been leaning toward all along
    D. It brought wrong associations (Gen. 19:1)
        1. He actually became part of what he was moving toward
        2. The worst part of it was that he knew it was wrong all the time (2 Peter 2:6–8)

II. **The Signs of His Backsliding**
    A. Turning away from godly influences
        1. He turned away from godly Abraham
        2. We turn from such influences as the Word, prayer, the church, Christian associations, etc.
    B. Living on the edge of the world
        1. He got close to it without getting into it—at first
        2. Many want to be as close to the edge as possible without falling out
    C. Adopting the ways of the world
        1. There was a measure of this in his encounter with the angels
        2. He tended to become like those with whom he associated
    D. Placing gain above God
        1. His temptation was not even very intense—he simply chose gain

2. We are sometimes sorely tempted in the choice between godliness and gain
E. Elevating the unsaved and unspiritual
   1. He lived with and among the ungodly
   2. He allowed their influence to shape his life

III. The Sorrows of His Backsliding
A. He lost his testimony—this is demonstrated by the lack of respect shown him by the men of the community (Gen. 19:5)
B. He lost his senses (Gen. 19:8)
   1. This is shown by his offer of his daughters to the perverted men of the community
   2 There are really no mitigating factors here
C. He lost his influence (Gen. 19:14b)
   1. His sons-in-law would not listen to him
   2. He actually lost his family as a result
D. He lost his possessions
   1. He left town with the clothing on his back
   2. It was desire for gain that led him astray in the first place
E. He lost his wife
   1. She was not really with him
   2. It appears her turning back was more than mere curiosity
F. He lost his spiritual sensitivity (Gen. 19:18–20)
   1. He stands and argues with the Lord
   2. He eventually has to abandon what he argued with the Lord about in the first place
G. He lost his own virtue and that of his daughters
   1. He ends in drunken incest
   2. We don't hear of him again, and he likely died a broken man

IV. The Solution to His Backsliding
A. "The Lord being merciful to him . . ." (Gen. 19:16)
   1. This mercy was the result of the intercession of Abraham
   2. He, himself, could lay claim to nothing
B. He was "saved like as by fire" (1 Cor. 3:15)

Conclusion:
This man made such a mess of things that we would question his salvation were it not for the fact that Peter refers to him as "righteous Lot." What a sad way to live and end a life. His life cries out to us, "Turn back from where you are on the road down!"

The High and the Mighty
Romans 12:3

Introduction:
Some believe all sin is pride. That may be debatable, but pride is surely sin. The book of Proverbs abounds with teaching (mostly warning) about pride (see Prov. 6:17; 8:13; 11:2; 13:10; 14:3; 15:25; 16:5, 18–19; 21:24; 28:25; 29:23).

I. **What Is Pride?**
    Pride is an inflated sense of one's own worth and relative importance. It is defined as "inordinate and unreasonable self-esteem, attended with insolence and rude treatment of others. It is an attempt to appear in a superior light."

II. **How Does Pride Operate?**
    A. It believes it is always right
    B. It can't bring itself to say, "I was wrong"
    C. It is easily offended
    D. It won't ask for assistance
    E. It tramples on others
    F. It readily becomes self-righteous
    G. It interferes in the affairs of others
    H. It specializes in unsolicited advice
    I. It elevates opinions into beliefs and convictions
    J. It views self as better than others
    K. It easily becomes involved in rebellion
    L. It knowingly disobeys God
    M. It is insensitive to the feelings of others
    N. It frequently boasts and brags
    O. It runs roughshod over others

III. **What Does Pride Do?**
    A. It antagonizes God
    B. It stunts spiritual growth
    C. It lessens spiritual effectiveness
    D. It damages relationships
    E. It clouds judgment
    F. It sets one up for failure

IV. **How Is Pride Conquered?**
    A. By recognizing that "I am a serious sinner. If no one else had ever sinned, my sin would have required the Cross"

B. By recognizing that "I am a potential disaster. I am capable of doing some incredible things apart from God's grace"
C. By recognizing that "I am constantly threatened. I am always on the brink of falling into sin"
D. By recognizing that "I am totally impotent. The only meaningful epitaph for my grave can be, 'Only a sinner saved by grace'"
E. By recognizing that "I am ultimately indebted. The only thing I have of any real value is my salvation, and I did nothing to gain that"
F. By recognizing that "I am completely dependent. Everything I have, including those things that I have earned with my hands and brain, traces back to Him and is a free gift from God"
G. By recognizing that "I am utterly equal. I am no better than anyone else, and there are people of far lower status than I who are my superiors in character, spirituality, etc."
H. By recognizing that "I am incorrigibly human. I am infinitely inferior to God even though I often act as if I were His superior"
I. By recognizing that "I am significantly self-deceived. I have weaknesses evident to everyone but me"
J. By recognizing that "I am unexposed. There are things in my life that, if known, would humiliate me"

Conclusion:

Don't worry about your self-concept or how to improve it. According to Scripture, it is already pretty good and needs little work. In fact, the real problem we face is pride and its effects.

God's Driving School
Exodus 14

Introduction:
Some people get lost without even trying; it is usually, however, because they didn't follow directions. Let's face it! You can follow the directions and still have problems, but they are not as likely. Here are some directions from God's Word to keep us straight in life.

I.   **Turn (vv. 1–4)**
    A. Sketch the history to this point
    B. There was a direct way to the Promised Land
    C. God told Moses to lead them away from it (to the South rather than to the East)
    D. Word got back to Pharaoh: "They are lost; we can catch them"
    E. God led them to an incredibly difficult place
    F. A tight spot proves nothing about the will of God
        1. It may be the result of personal foolishness
        2. It may be the result of the will of the Lord

II.   **Stop (vv. 10–14)**
    A. Describe the situation
    B. Other voices were calling to them
        1. Despair—complain, quit, and die
        2. Cowardice—retreat, take up again the yoke of bondage
        3. Precipitancy—take action, make haste, "do something"
        4. Presumption—figure it out, take the matter in hand
    C. God's word—"stand still"
        1. He was working out higher purposes
            a. The destruction of Egypt
            b. A nation, a free nation, in just seven days
        2. An active standing in trust, in prayer, in expectancy, in readiness (this is how to wait when you don't know what to do)

III. **Go (vv. 15–31)**
    A. At the proper moment, God gave Moses a command
    B. They were to go forward
        1. Notice the direction—forward
        2. Movement not completely clear

3. Movement a bit shaky
4. Movement required faith—they couldn't see the end from the beginning
C. When God says to move—move!
D. When you do know what to do, *do it!* Broader concept here: Don't stop when you know what to do—just do it

Conclusion:

You may be at the Red Sea right now as a result of your own foolishness or even actually in the will of God. If you don't know what to do, stand still and see the salvation of God. If you do know what to do, do it! Move forward when God says move, even though you can't see the entire outcome. Above all, be sure you are related to the God who gives directions.

Walking Slowly, Talking Softly, Kicking Stones
Philippians 2:12–16

Introduction:
This passage contains some surprises. It is significantly more meaningful when it is viewed from the proper perspective. It says, "Do all things without murmurings [grumbling] and disputings [dialogue]" (v. 14).

I.   **The Context**
    A. You work out your salvation—in the sense of the implications of that salvation
    B. God works in you His will
        1. He expresses His will
        2. He orders your circumstances
    C. Do all things without
        1. Murmurings—outward expressions of inward dissatisfactions
        2. Disputings—dialogues, debates, discussions, etc.
    D. So that you will have a good testimony
    E. So that Paul's labor will not have been in vain

II. **The Caution**
    A. A serious matter (1 Cor. 10:1–10)
    B. A blasphemous matter (Exod. 16:8)
    C. A dangerous matter (Num. 14:27–29)

III. **The Content**
    A. Against the dealings of God (Phil. 2:12–13)
    B. Against the providence of God—the way of God in directing His people (Exod. 16:1–3)
    C. Against the provision of God (Exod. 16:1–3)
    D. Against the purposes of God—Romans 8:28 didn't appear out of nowhere in the New Testament. It was already prefigured in Numbers 14:36
    E. Against the messengers of God (Num. 14:2)
    F. Against the commandments of God (Num. 27:14)
    G. Against the freedom of God—God in His sovereignty is absolutely free to deal with anyone as He so wishes, and the very fact He does so in a certain way indicates that that way is just and equitable (Matt. 20:1–16)

IV. **The Challenge**
    A. God's ways are perfect
        1. Deuteronomy 32:4

2. 2 Samuel 22:31, 33
3. Psalm 18:30, 32
B. Our response is to be one of silent submission
   1. There is some emphasis today on being angry with God
   2. There is no place in Scripture for anger with God
   3. This is exactly what this passage is teaching

Conclusion:

We must take Romans 8:28 and Philippians 2:14 together! God does not want to argue with men. He wants men to listen to Him and do what He says. Reasoning that begins to express itself externally can become murmuring. How are you doing on accepting what God is doing in your life?

Like a Tree

2 Peter 3:18

Introduction:

Growth is expected in life, and we are troubled by lack of physical growth. We tend to be equally troubled by lack of emotional growth. What ought to be more troubling, however, is the lack of spiritual growth. An old commentator has said, "Ordinarily men in religion are what they design to be. They have about as much religion as they wish, and possess about the character that they intend to possess."

I. **Spiritual Growth Is Likened to a Tree**
    A. We must grow downward—getting roots down deep
    B. We must grow upward—perfecting our relationship with the Lord
    C. We must grow outward—ever spreading our influence abroad
    D. We must bear fruit—such is a clear sign of health

II. **Spiritual Growth Is a Continuing Process**
    A. There is no chance of perfection on earth
        1. No one has ever grown as much as he or she could
        2. Few have ever grown as much as they should
    B. The process must be a constant concern
        1. We grow or we decline—a plateau is a decline
        2. How much thought and effort do you give to growth?

III. **Spiritual Growth Is the Result of Specific Effort**
    A. We are commanded to do it
    B. Growth is not something that just happens to us
    C. Note the difference between physical and emotional growth
        1. Physical growth just happens
        2. Emotional growth comes through effort

IV. **Spiritual Growth Is the Product of a Program**
    A. It comes from exposure to the Word
    B. It comes from practicing the Word
    C. It comes from applying the Word to life

V. **Spiritual Growth Involves Struggle**
    A. Satan always opposes growth
    B. Some growth comes through the struggle

1. We don't like the problems in our spiritual lives
2. Spiritual problems often lead to growth

VI. Spiritual Growth Is Always Measurable
  A. We tend to measure growth in terms of growth in knowledge
    1. This may be the biggest problem in Christianity
    2. Truth is meaningless if it is not applied
  B. It should be measured in terms of conformity to Christ
    1. Since we are not naturally like that, growth involves change
    2. Change becomes a valid measurement of growth

Conclusion:

Are you as old as you actually are? Does your maturity level match your chronology? Are you as old as you actually are spiritually? What needs work? Someone has said, "Growth shall prove your life."

What Shall We Then Say?

Romans 8:31–35

Introduction:

In Romans 8:1–30, Paul deals with the adequacy of the grace of God to meet the needs of man. In Romans 8:31–39, Paul deals with the adequacy of the God of grace to meet the needs of man.

I. **What Are "These Things"?**
   A. The phrase refers to everything else in the chapter
   B. The adequacy of the grace of God for the problems of man
      1. The guilt and power of sin (vv. 1–9)
      2. The inevitable fact of death (vv. 6–13)
      3. The terror of God's holiness (v. 15)
      4. The problem of suffering (vv. 17–25)
      5. Problems in prayer (v. 26ff.)
      6. Feelings of hopelessness (vv. 26–27)
   C. The gifts of God given to the sons of God
      1. Righteousness (v. 1); "no condemnation"
      2. The Holy Spirit (vv. 4–27)
      3. Sonship (adoption) (vv. 14–17, 29)
      4. Security (vv. 28–30)
      5. This provides us status + dynamic + identity + safe-conduct

II. **What Shall We Then Say to Them? (Note that the answers to this question are themselves questions)**
   A. No one can succeed against us (v. 31b)
      1. "If God be for us . . ."—since God is for us
      2. This does not mean that people won't try
      3. This truth is due to our relationship: "my father is bigger than your father"
   B. No good thing will be held back from us (v. 32)
      1. He has already given us the ultimate gift—His own Son, given freely
      2. If He has already given us the ultimate, why not everything else?
      3. This deals with the things we really need
   C. No charge can ever stand against us (v. 33)
      1. This raises the issue of Satan's accusations
      2. Such accusations have no impact! Nothing can be brought that He doesn't know or hasn't cared for

3. This ministers to the tenderhearted souls that are always losing the sense of God's love
   D. No separation can ever befall us (v. 35)
      1. One of the clearest statements of Scripture
      2. Divine love has at its heart an almighty purpose to bless that cannot be thwarted
      3. You are not strong enough to fall away while God holds you

III. **What Does This All Mean to Us?**
   A. It assures us of our security in Christ
      1. God established the bond—nothing can break it
      2. It does not give us a license to do wrong; that view is perverted
   B. It confirms our confidence in verse 28
      1. What more could happen to us than is covered by these four questions?
      2. The God who has this much invested in us will surely care for us
   C. It emphasizes our factual foundation
      1. Biblical Christianity is based upon facts, and as such is logical
      2. Man's desire—and much of the basis of modern religion—is feeling

Conclusion:

It is foolish to eschew doctrine, as chapters such as this are full of doctrine. Remember, great doctrinal truths always have meaning and application. It all comes down to one simple truth: "The best measure of a spiritual life is not ecstasies, but obedience" (Oswald Chambers).

Stop That!

Psalm 37:27

Introduction:

There are a lot of stress producers mentioned in this chapter: evil doers (v. 1), need and inadequacies (v. 3), the fleeting satisfactions of life (v. 4), the uncertainties and difficulties of life (v. 5), the upsetting and unexplainable things of life (v. 7), and emotional overload, especially with anger (v. 8). Verse 27 deals with the stress caused by self-created situations.

I. **The Problem**
   A. Much of our stress is self-produced
      1. By wrong choices
      2. By wrong actions
      3. By wrong thinking
   B. Many of our most stressful situations are ones into which we managed to get ourselves. Much of our other stress is caused by our reactions to life

II. **The Prescription**
   A. "Depart from evil"
      1. *Evil* is a fairly general name for wrong
      2. This is a comprehensive commandment
         a. Do nothing that is wrong
         b. Break no laws of God
         c. Violate no command of conscience; have a conscience devoid of offense to self, man, God
      3. "Depart"—break off from the practice and abjure the love of that which is wrong
   B. "Do good"
      1. *Good* is a general term for that which is right, proper
      2. This is also a comprehensive commandment
         a. Actively perform the will of God from the heart
         b. Discharge every known duty
         c. Practice every revealed virtue
         d. Carry out the precepts of the moral law in every possible particular
      3. "Do"—engage in the serious practice of godliness
   C. The combination
      1. Provides a "put-off/put-on" combination
      2. We best put off doing evil by beginning to do good
      3. This is the basic rule of the Christian life (Ps. 34:14)

III. The Product
    A. "Dwell for evermore"
    B. Blessing to Israel—"If you depart from evil and do good, you will dwell in the land forever"
    C. The result to us of departing from evil and doing good will be peace and long life

IV. The Point
    A. Two things are in view here:
        1. These things will keep you out of stress
        2. These things will help you out of stress
    B. The process to follow when in trouble
        1. Identify how you got into the trouble
        2. Stop doing what it was that got you there
        3. Replace the wrong with a right
        4. Undo, where possible, the effects of the wrong
        5. Don't do another wrong on top of the first one
    C. If following these commands creates stress, turn that over to God as it is His special responsibility

Conclusion:

Much of our stress is from messes we make for ourselves. When you become aware that such is the case, take action: turn aside from doing evil; pick up on doing that which is good. "No truce is to be made or parley held with sin! We must turn away from it without hesitation, and set ourselves practically to work in the opposite direction" (C. H. Spurgeon).

Flared Nostrils and a Poisonous Fever

Psalm 37:8

Introduction:

There is likely nothing more stress producing than anger. There are two kinds of anger, and both are dangerous: expressed anger produces stress; internalized anger has the same effect. This is why Solomon said, "Make no friendship with an angry man; and with a furious man thou shalt not go" (Prov. 22:24). Here's a look at anger from a biblical perspective.

I. **The Reasons for Anger**
   A. Selfishness causes about 90 percent of all our anger
      1. "You got in my way"
      2. "You kept me from getting my way"
      3. "You made me look bad"
      4. "You intruded on my privacy"
   B. Anger and the issue of self-concept
      1. Anger is usually attributed to poor self-concept
      2. Anger is actually a matter of good self-concept; if my self-concept really were poor, you wouldn't be able to bother me with what you do
   C. Unselfish anger
      1. Some anger is in the realm of righteous indignation
      2. The anger of Christ comes under this heading
      3. Actually, there is not too much of this among Christians

II. **The Results of Anger**
   A. Internal turmoil
      1. Regret
      2. Guilt
      3. Physical implications
   B. Damaged relationships
      1. Wounded feelings
      2. Fear
      3. Bitterness
   C. Undermined testimony—before saved and unsaved alike

III. **The Resolution of Anger**
   A. Recognize the commandment
      1. Note the double commandment here
      2. Note the specific meanings: anger is from a word that means "nostrils flared in anger"; wrath is from a word that means "poisoned" from fever

B. Accept individual responsibility
C. Confess your sin
D. Admit personal possibility
E. Reevaluate your self-importance
F. Submit to His sovereignty
G. Refuse to succumb to your weakness
H. Make yourself accountable
I. Provide some built-in restraint
J. Don't be defeated by failure

Conclusion:

Many people live their lives in anger, while others have periodic problems with it. The Bible lays responsibility for it on us, but it also produces a possibility for us. We need to hear and heed, "Wherefore . . . let every man be swift to hear, slow to speak, slow to wrath: For the wrath of man worketh not the righteousness of God" (James 1:20).

Life's Tough

Psalm 37:5–6

Introduction:

There's no escaping it; life's tough! The most difficult thing that most Christians face is living daily life as Christians ought to live, and most of us experience some stress as part of daily living.

I. **The Cause of Our Stress**
    A. Our inability
        1. Our world is complex and confusing
        2. Our Bible is complete and sufficient
        3. We often have trouble relating these two facts
    B. Life's uncertainty
        1. Few things are really certain in life
        2. We face uncertainty daily
        3. Uncertainty is very stressful
    C. Other's opposition
        1. It piles up on top of our inability and uncertainty
        2. It makes us much more unsure of ourselves
        3. It is difficult to handle even where we are sure of our course as it can involve lies, slander, or just severe criticism

II. **The Cure for Our Stress**
    A. "Commit"
        1. Meaning "roll over or on to" (clarified in Gen. 29:3, 8, 10)
        2. Expressed in Psalm 55:22; Proverbs 16:3; 1 Peter 5:7
        3. "Thy way"—course of life, mode of operation, entire path of life
    B. "Trust"
        1. A strong sense of security, find confidence in
        2. "Hie to" as a place of refuge
        3. Note again the importance of the object of our trust
    C. Applied—doesn't involve total passivity
        1. Do what you can or are supposed to do
        2. Then put your trust in Him
        3. Leave the results in His care
        4. Expect a positive outcome

III. **The Certainties in Our Stress**
    A. "He shall bring it to pass"
        1. He will bring things to a proper issue
        2. This is Old Testament for Romans 8:28

    B. He will vindicate your action
        1. "He shall bring forth thy righteousness"
        2. He will bring out your rightness as a reassurance to you that doing right is worthwhile

Conclusion:

    There are three lessons to learn here: (1) In the face of inability and uncertainty, "Our destiny shall be joyfully accomplished if we confidently entrust all to our Lord" (C. H. Spurgeon); (2) in the face of lies and slander, "If we look to His honor, He will see to ours"; (3) in the face of seeing evildoers appear to prosper, "Fret not! Sooner or later, God will cause your light to shine forth." Life's tough, but there is an answer: Do what you know to do and then roll it on the Lord.

Less Stress and More Rest

Psalm 37

Introduction:
There are two true statements: (1) "There is no such thing as stress"; (2) "stress is a major factor in our society." Stress does not exist as a tangible entity; you can't package it or buy it or even say for sure that certain things are stressful. Actually, stress is a measure of our internal reaction to the stimuli of life. Because it is internal, it is self-produced. Stress is not inherent in anything. Some things provide more potential for it, but one man's pressure cooker is another's picnic.

I. **The Problem**
    A. This psalm deals with the problem of wicked people
        1. Their prosperity
        2. Their actions
        3. Their "getting away with murder"
        4. Their determinate opposition to right
    B. The psalm deals with the problem of wicked people as they present conditions for stress
        1. This truth is probably more germane to certain times
        2. Came from David's experience
    C. There is more here than just the problem of wicked people
        1. It provides general principles for handling upset
        2. It treats the whole subject admirably

II. **The Prescription—There are eight precepts given in the passage**
    A. "Fret not" (v. 1)—don't let your engine boil over
    B. "Trust in the Lord, and do good" (v. 3)—a form of "Trust and Obey"
    C. "Delight thyself also in the Lord" (v. 4)—find your satisfaction in Him
    D. "Commit thy way unto the Lord" (v. 5)—turn your life over to His control
    E. "Rest in the Lord" (v. 7)—relax in the care of your Father
    F. "Cease from anger" (v. 8)—stop getting angry about everything
    G. "Depart from evil, and do good" (v. 27)—a two-pronged direction

H. "Wait on the Lᴏʀᴅ" (v. 34)—wait *for* the Lord

I. Properly understood and applied, these are stress reducers or eliminators

III. The Proposals

A. Some stress is germane to the human state and the old nature

  1. Some is a patterned response
  2. Some is because it is expected of us
  3. Some is for excuse purposes

B. Stress is the result of failing to react to the stimuli of life in a biblical manner

  1. Some is the result of specific disobedience
  2. Stress is a choice!

C. Following the procedures laid out here would result in a vast reduction in stress

  1. Our big difficulty is in accepting that
     a. God knows what is going on
     b. God knows what He is doing
     c. God is able to do what needs doing
     d. God may not happen to agree with me on what is best or how things ought to be done
  2. We have trouble allowing God to be God, and the result is stress

Conclusion:

God has made provision for less stress and more rest, but the choice is yours. What will you choose?

Spirituality

James 4:7–10

Introduction:

James has been dealing with a couple of problems in the church. In 4:1–3 he deals with the subject of self-centeredness, and in 4:4–6 he deals with the issue of worldliness. He now turns to the antidote—that which can cure the problems of self-centeredness and worldliness—and tells us that it is genuine spirituality.

I. **"Submit Yourself to God" (v. 7a)**
   A. Voluntarily place yourself under God
   B. This is not at all subjective
      1. Obey His Word
      2. Accept His dealings (the unchangeable)
   C. Beware—it has been said, "In order to know the will of God, I must have no will of my own"; the contrary is actually true, "My will must be to do His will"

II. **"Resist the Devil" (v. 7b)—"Take a Stand Against" (military term)**
   A. Recognize that you don't have to fall to him
   B. Be aware of his devices ("for we are not ignorant of . . ." [2 Chron. 2:11])
   C. Avoid his contamination
      1. Reject his appeals (subtle philosophy)
      2. "Just say no" to his blandishments

III. **"Draw Nigh to God" (vv. 8–9)**
   A. Change your focus
      1. Turn your attention toward
      2. Set your affections on (involves thinking on)
      3. The means are Bible study, prayer, church, etc.
   B. Deal with your sin—"Cleanse your hands, ye sinners"
      1. Ceremonial cleansing in view here
      2. Symbolic of dealing with actual sinful actions
   C. Deal with your mind-set—"Purify your hearts, ye double minded"
      1. Get rid of what is behind your sinful conduct
      2. Symbolic of dealing with your thinking—philosophy
   D. Deal with your attitude—"Be afflicted, and mourn, and weep"
      1. Treat sin as something serious
      2. Self-imposed sorrow that is wrapped up with repentance

E. Deal with your approach to life—laughter into mourning and joy into pain
   1. Don't be guilty of a frivolous treatment of sin
   2. Turn your self-satisfied joy to gloom (real joy comes after, as a result of change in one's approach to life)

IV. Humble Yourselves in the Sight of the Lord (v. 10)
A. This involves getting a proper view of yourself
   1. See yourself for what you are
   2. See the source of everything you have
   3. Recognize what you are able to do (to fail to do so is to engage in false humility)
   4. Recognize what you are unable to do (or not supposed to do) and stop trying to do it.
B. The result will be exaltation from God rather than self advancement

Conclusion:
Spirituality is not a great secret! Biblical spirituality is not popular because it is very specific, and it is easier to make subjective commitments than it is to obey the specific commands of Scripture. Genuine spirituality will take care of self-centeredness and worldliness.

Talking Pottery?
Isaiah 45:9–12

Introduction:
If you were told that an inanimate object could speak to you, you would say, "Why, that's preposterous." Yes, but not the most preposterous thing ever heard. The most preposterous statement is in this passage.

I. **The Reproof**
    A. The situation
        1. God had predicted hard times for the Jews
        2. He had told them of impending captivity
        3. He had promised them ultimate restoration
        4. Now He hit them with an indication that a Gentile would lead that restoration (vv. 1–4)
    B. The statement—"Woe unto him"
        1. Means "look out, beware"
        2. It is directed to the one who challenges God. It is not necessarily wrong to question God, but it is wrong to challenge Him, which is what is in view here
        3. "Striveth with"—has controversy with
    C. The striving
        1. Means to argue with, to resist
        2. It also covers complaint, murmuring
    D. The sameness
        1. Israel was very good at this
        2. We are all prone to it at times (anytime we argue with God or refuse to accept His will for us or our situation)

II. **The Reasons (Why Such Striving Is Wrong)**
    A. Because it is a form of rebellion against God
    B. Because it is an act of ingratitude
    C. Because it is almost always selfish
        1. We only fuss when things don't go our way
        2. We'd rather others suffer than us
    D. Because it demonstrates pride
        1. It shows we don't see ourselves as we are
        2. It shows we feel we need no chastening
    E. Because it is an act of disobedience
    F. Because it is really absurd
    G. Because it is inconsistent with our own beliefs

H. Because it is ignorant
I. Because it is shortsighted (it sees things only in terms of time)
J. Because it is basically vain

III. The Remedy
    A. Recognition
        1. The foolishness of what we are doing
        2. This passage is designed to do that very thing
    B. React properly
        1. David (Ps. 119:73)
        2. Job (Job 13:15)
        3. Joseph (Gen. 50:12)
    C. Respond positively
        1. God knows best
        2. God is working things according to a plan
        3. We gain most by working with His program

Conclusion:

It is foolish for man to strive with God. It is most foolish in areas such as salvation. God has already determined what will work and has structured everything to that end. We are not going to change His mind. Are you striving with God? Are you doing things God's way?

The Genuine Article
Psalm 15

Introduction:
What is the easiest way to tell if an item is counterfeit? Comparison to the real thing. God shows us here what the real thing is in regard to Christianity so we can compare ourselves—and others after ourselves—to it.

I. **"He Whose Walk Is Blameless" (v. 2 NIV)**
   A. "Blameless" not "perfect"
   B. Not "no charges," but no charges that stick
   C. His life is complete, all essential aspects of character are present

II. **"[He] Who Does What Is Righteous" (v. 2 NIV)**
   A. He practices rectitude
   B. The man who puts integrity into his life
   C. No man is worthy to be called a friend of God who does not habitually do that which is right

III. **"[He] Who Speaks the Truth from His Heart" (v. 2 NIV)**
   A. Sincerity as opposed to outward show or mere profession
   B. The truth dwells in his heart, and he speaks it there first before he expresses it with his tongue
   C. He speaks truth because he loves truth; it has been said, "Truth is God's daughter"

IV. **"[He] Who Has No Slander on His Tongue" (v. 3 NIV)**
   A "He who has no slander"—and what he says reveals his character in the normal course of life
   B. This is from the Hebrew word "to foot it"
   C. Described
      1. Slow to believe evil of another
      2. Does not find pleasure in evil
      3. Does not originate evil report
      4. Does not readily affirm such when spoken by others
      5. Believes evil report only in the face of overwhelming evidence
      6. Believes evil report, when forced, contrary to the desires of his heart

V. "[He] Who Does His Neighbor No Wrong" (v. 3 NIV)

A. This phrase adds deed to word

B. "He who bridles his tongue will not give a license to his hand" (C. H. Spurgeon)

VI. "[He Who] Casts No Slur on His Fellow Man" (v. 3 NIV)

A. This speaks of scandal, reproach, defamatory accusation

B. He does not pick up on what has been said about his neighbor (cf. Prov. 26:17)

C. He doesn't transmit or add to what has been said

VII. "[He] Who Despises a Vile Man but Honors Those Who Fear the LORD" (v. 4 NIV)

A. He despises and honors properly (Isa. 5:20)

B. He only honors those who are honorable

C. He does not show respect to a man of base or bad character on account of his wealth, his position, or his rank in life

D. He doesn't hesitate to express his despite

VIII. "[He] Who Keeps His Oath Even When It Hurts" (v. 4 NIV)

A. He has sworn in a way that will injure himself, but he will not substitute something for what he has promised

B. Converse is also true—he will break a wrong commitment even if it costs him something significant

IX. "[He] Who Lends His Money Without Usury" (v. 4 NIV)

A. Commercial lending was unknown then

B. This has to do with usurious lending to the poor or to one's spiritual brother

C. The basic meaning—he who does not take advantage of those in distress

X. "[He] Who Does Not Accept a Bribe Against the Innocent" (v. 5 NIV)

A. Common in many places to bribe in justice area

B. This man will not allow his justice and equity to be tampered with by anyone

Conclusion:

One can tell a counterfeit by comparison. This is true of people as well as things. Just as a bill may be a bit defaced and still genuine, God can see the same with people.

Integrity
Proverbs 11:3; 19:1; 20:7

Introduction:
   Training in counseling often teaches that some people are so lacking in some aspect of character that they can be accurately described as having a hole in their character. It seems this hole is often in the realm of integrity.

I.   **Integrity Is an Inner Quality**
   A.   This is obvious in Job (27:5; 31:6)
   B.   It is a combination of qualities
      1.   Truthfulness—speech
      2.   Honesty—actions
      3.   Sincerity—spirit and attitude

II.   **Integrity Affects the Way One Lives**
   A.   Proverbs 11:3
   B.   It determines
      1.   Manner of life
      2.   Specific decisions
      3.   Operations in all areas

III.   **Integrity Is of Priceless Worth**
   A.   Proverbs 19:1
   B.   It is greater than things we usually value most
      1.   It taints everything when absent
      2.   It paints everything when it is present

IV.   **Integrity Measures What a Man Really Is**
   A.   Lack of any one aspect of character creates a hole in the whole composition
   B.   The word has an essential meaning of "whole, complete, entire"
   C.   Without it, a person is lacking

V.   **Integrity Can Be Obtained**
   A.   It is not natural
   B.   There are great hindrances to it
      1.   Self-preservation
      2.   Self-provision
      3.   Self-promotion
   C.   It is best developed by exposure to the Word

Conclusion:
   The greatest distance between the pulpit and the pew often lies in the application of what is preached. Do you live what is preached? Integrity equals completeness. Are you complete?

A Clear Conscience

Acts 23:1; 24:16

Introduction:
The word *conscience* comes from two words: *con* equals "with" and *science* equals "knowledge." It has the idea of self knowledge. Thus, a *clear* conscience would be one that knows nothing against itself and that always acts in accord with its own beliefs.

I. **The Importance of a Clear Conscience**
    A. Paul illustrates the concept here
    B. Note that
        1. Paul was willing to abide by commands he didn't agree with
        2. Modern Christians often even overthrow their own beliefs in their quest for freedom

II. **The Inadequacy of a Clear Conscience**
    A. We can have a clear conscience and still do wrong—after all, Paul had consented to stoning Stephen
    B. Conscience is easily conditioned

III. **The Instruction of Conscience (1 Cor. 4:4)**
    A. Conscience must be instructed
    B. The only truly valid conscience is one submitted to the Word of God
        1. The ultimate test—not, "Do I act in accord with my beliefs" but "Do I believe right?"
        2. To pride self on not being a hypocrite is not very meaningful

IV. **The Implications of a Clear Conscience**
    A. It is a matter of effort—I practice
    B. It is bidirectional—God/man
    C. It involves
        1. Not being aware of acting out of accord with biblically-based beliefs
        2. Having confessed anything out of accord
        3. Having made wrongs right

Conclusion:
There are always reasons why we don't clear our consciences. Those reasons are seldom what we tell ourselves and others. The reasons are usually one or more of three: pride, rebellion, or we're not through with that sin just yet. Is your conscience clear?

Wait on the Lord
Proverbs 20:22b

Introduction:
There are few things most of us like less than waiting, but waiting is a necessary part of spiritual experience. *Waiting* is used eighty-five times in the Old Testament, and six different Hebrew words are translated *wait*. We always face the question of how long should I wait, and when should I act? Let's look at the subject of waiting on the Lord.

I.   **Why Should We Wait on the Lord?**
   A.   We should wait for strength—Psalm 27:14
      1.   Our strength is always inadequate
      2.   Our strength pales in comparison to His
      3.   His strength is always available
   B.   We should wait for provision of needs—Psalm 37:34
      1.   This is a matter of things we really must have
      2.   It involves the supply of every legitimate need
      3.   The supply comes from His hand
   C.   We should wait for blessing—Psalm 37:34
      1.   This is a broader term—needs and things beyond needs
      2.   We need some things in life that only God can do
      3.   His blessing is perfection (makes rich without regrets)
   D.   We should wait for defense—Proverbs 20:22
      1.   The best defense is from the Lord
      2.   This is hardest of all for us to do
      3.   We should do what is right and allow God to take care of it
   E.   We should wait for renewal—Isaiah 40:31
      1.   This is primarily spiritual, but it is not limited to the spiritual
      2.   This takes into account the wearying nature of life and its demands
      3.   He makes an incredible promise here

II. **How Should We Wait on the Lord?**
   A.   By standing before Him—Psalm 25:5
      1.   This has the idea of being in His presence
      2.   This stresses the continual need for spiritual life and growth

B. By looking to Him for our supply—Psalm 25:3
   1. This has reference to prayer
   2. It means to keep things before Him as our divine source
C. By tarrying before Him—Psalm 37:7
   1. By continuing to keep things before Him
   2. By taking time to develop the relationship
D. By being silent before Him—Psalm 62:5
   1. This involves allowing Him to speak to us (primarily through and always in accord with the Word)
   2. This involves allowing Him to shape our requests, etc.
E. By confidently expecting from Him—Psalm 33:22
   1. All the words for "wait" have an expectation aspect
   2. We should anticipate His response, or what's the point of waiting?

III. **How Does This Relate to Our Lives?**
   A. Stay before the Lord
      1. It ought to be part of daily life
      2. It ought to be particularly true in trouble
      3. There is no substitute for this
   B. Stand still before the Lord
      1. This is not an excuse for inaction
      2. More mistakes are made by haste than by waiting
      3. The ultimate responsibility is not ours
   C. Keep the matter before the Lord
      1. Keep on praying until the prayer is answered or the burden is lifted
      2. God has timing as well as response in mind
      3. Don't give up and get discouraged
   D. Expect something from God
      1. Faith involves expectation
      2. The real question is often not *if* God will answer but *how* and *when* He will answer
      3. Claim His promises when faith falters

Conclusion:

We have the sentence of death in ourselves to teach us not to trust in ourselves but in God. Waiting on the Lord comes in exactly at this point. We all do well at being upset, having needs, crying out, and so forth. How well are you doing at waiting on the Lord?

The Things Most Difficult

Isaiah 40:31

Introduction:
What is the most difficult thing you have to do? Is it to get up and go to work in the morning? To keep calm when your kids are acting up? To tell someone "no"? To face the bill collector when you don't have the money? To care for an aged loved one? Here are some other suggestions.

I. **Life's Difficulties**
    A. Difficult things to do
        1. Conduct funerals for friends
        2. Counsel when it isn't wanted
        3. Peacemaking
        4. Confrontation
    B. Difficult things to experience
        1. Financial shortages
        2. Anyone leaving one's "circle"
        3. Rebuffs in witnessing
        4. Things that won't "fit together"
    C. Difficult things to endure
        1. Indifference when revival is needed
        2. Lies that cannot be refuted
        3. The defection of trusted friends
        4. The loss of a lifetime love

II. **Life's Greatest Difficulty—Nothing**
    A. The hardest thing to do is nothing
        1. This is especially true when something needs to be done, or I want to do something
        2. This bothered God's people in Scripture—they had to be told to stand still (Exod. 14:13; Num. 9:8; 1 Sam. 12:7)
        3. God sometimes says, "Don't just do something, stand there!"
    B. The hardest thing to experience is nothing
        1. We struggle with times when nothing is happening
        2. This appears to have troubled Solomon (Eccl. 1:9–11)
        3. More people fall as a result of nothing than of something (impatience makes us vulnerable)
        4. Most people who fall in a time of crisis have already fallen when there was no crisis

C. The hardest thing to endure is nothing
   1. This is especially applied to times when prayer is not answered
   2. David appears to have struggled with this (Ps. 69:3)
   3. We travel by jet; God walks!

III. **The Answer to These Difficulties—Wait on the Lord**
   A. *Wait*—"To stay in a place or remain in readiness or in anticipation (until something expected happens or for someone to arrive or catch up); to remain or delay in anticipation or expectation"
   B. More than eighteen words in the Bible are translated as *wait*
      1. Most have the idea of "hope, expect, look for"
      2. Some have a strong note of "be silent, patient"
   C. Guidelines for that which runs contrary to our nature
      1. When you know what to do based on the Word and prayer, then do it
      2. When you don't know what to do, don't do anything until you do know what to do or you must do something
      3. When you turn something over to the Lord, allow Him time to work it out
      4. Generally speaking, be quicker to wait than to act
   D. The ultimate answer (Isa. 40:31)
      1. *Wait* in this place has the sense of "being entwined with." Get so entwined with Him that the strength, etc., comes from Him at all times
      2. We wait much more easily when we are really wrapped up with Him

Conclusion:

George Muller wrote in his Bible, "The steps of a good man . . ."; and added the notation, "and the stops too." Phillips Brooks once said, "The trouble is that I'm in a hurry, and God isn't." Don't forget: "Ye have need of patience that after ye have done the will of God you might receive the promise" (Heb. 10:36).

Changed!

2 Corinthians 3:18

Introduction:

A young mother was once heard to say, "You are the hardest child to change." How often God must say this about Christians! What's so difficult about change?

I. **God Has a Purpose for Us**
   A. That purpose is to change us
      1. He is involved in making something out of us
      2. It is expressed in passages such as Ephesians 1:4 and 2:10
   B. That change is to be on the deepest level
      1. There are two words for change in the New Testament
      2. This one is "metamorphosis" or a radical, dynamic, internal change
   C. This is not what we are being told in our day
      1. Various life-purposes are set forth as positive
      2. Almost all such purposes are self-centered

II. **God Has a Pattern in His Purpose**
   A. That pattern is the image of His dear Son
      1. We are to be like Christ
      2. This is a process
   B. This verse means
      1. As we look at Him we are changed to become like Him
      2. This extends from the glory of salvation to the glory of glorification
   C. Everyone wants to change others (media, mental health practitioners, radical activists, etc.)
      1. Change is always in the direction the changer desires
      2. Only Christianity offers a fixed point of reference

III. **God Has a Plan to Pattern His Purpose**
   A. He works to change us, using
      1. Challenge—positive appeals to change that come from various sources
      2. Confrontation—this comes through the Bible, preachers, other people, and situations in which He brings us up short

3. Chastisement—when all else fails. God brings pressure to bear on our lives in a variety of ways and in increasing intensity
   B. He uses various other factors
      1. The calendar—the timing of things
      2. Circumstances—all the events of our lives are designed to make us what He wants us to be. This is how Romans 8:28–29 fits in
      3. Calamities—when we won't learn through other means, God sometimes brings calamity because it is better that something happen to us than that His purposes be thwarted

Conclusion:

God's purpose is change. God's pattern is likeness to Christ (what He wants us to be like). God's plan is to use whatever it takes to make the changes. How are you changing right now? How have you changed in recent days? What is God trying to change in your life? How are you cooperating?

All Things?

Philippians 4:10–19

Introduction:
It is very possible to read Scripture and to seize on a verse and interpret it without looking for its internal connection. Such action may result in taking a verse to mean what it does not mean. Philippians 4:13 is a case in point. It has most frequently been taken without reference to its context and, thus, a secondary meaning has been made primary. The result is that some tremendous teaching is missed.

I. **The Setting of the Verse**
   A. In a longer section on giving
   B. It actually relates to a shorter section (vv. 11–12)
      1. Paul's statement in verse 11
      2. Paul's experience in verse 12
   C. "I can do all things . . ." relates to what he has said in the previous two verses

II. **The Specifics of the Verse**
   A. He has talked about two conditions
      1. Abounding—being on top, having plenty
      2. Abased—being on the bottom, destitute
   B. He has talked about two actions
      1. Going suddenly from one to the other
      2. Bouncing around between the two points (almost to the point of experiencing both at the same time— "I am instructed . . .")
   C. He has talked about a single response
      1. "Content"
      2. "I can do all things [even be content in the face of such shifting circumstances] through Christ who enables me"

III. **The Stress of the Verse**
   A. Normal stress—"I can do anything that God wants me to do"
      1. For example, speak before five hundred people, stop biting my nails, break a bad moral habit
      2. This is a correct stress, but it is a secondary stress at best
   B. Proper stress—"I can face any circumstance and the changing circumstances of life by His power"

1. "I can endure" rather than "I can accomplish"
2. The nature of our lives is such that we need the promise of endurance more than the promise of accomplishment

IV. **The Solution in the Verse**
    A. How does the Lord enable me to face any circumstance and the changing circumstances of life?
      1. He enables me in answer to prayer
      2. He enables me through a mind-set
    B. What is the mind-set that will enable me to handle life?
      1. When down—"I deserve nothing"
        a. Most upset comes from disappointed expectations (the idea that we have something coming)
        b. It is best to remember the prominence of the concept of grace
      2. When up—"I possess nothing"
        a. Nothing I have is mine, so what if it is taken from me?
        b. Nothing I have was ultimately earned by me (it comes from God-given ability)
    C. This gives a clue to a broader application
      1. I can handle the bottom and the top; I can handle moving suddenly between the two; I can handle swinging wildly between the two
      2. If I can handle that, then I can handle anything

Conclusion:
This is a wonderful promise, but we have stripped it of some of its meaning by not seeing it in context. It's not just that I can do or cannot do certain things; it is that I can handle life—no matter what it may throw at me.

Never Overwhelmed!

1 Corinthians 10:13

Introduction:

Have you ever watched someone "walk away" from the faith? Have you ever felt that you couldn't take it any more? Have you ever been more frustrated by someone's "helpful" cliché or platitude? Have you ever wondered exactly what God was doing in your life? Paul has a word for all these situations!

I. **The Common Experience of All People**
   A. The meaning of temptation
      1. A solicitation to evil
      2. A specific form of trial
      3. The two concepts somewhat meet—that which pulls us away from God: the trial is often a temptation, while a temptation is always a trial
   B. "Such as is common to man"—human in its nature
      1. It is human to be tempted
      2. The temptations that come are suited to humans
      3. The temptations are like those of others

II. **The Special Dealings of God—"God is faithful"**
   A. He allows temptations
   B. He tailors temptations
      1. They are limited by our ability to survive
      2. They are limited by our ability to bear up under
   C. He sends a way to escape
      1. There is a way out of every temptation/testing
      2. We are responsible for discovering it
      3. We usually miss it because of hopelessness, grumbling, rebellion, wrong focus, etc.

III. **The Exceptional Situation of the Saints**
   A. They are tested as other men
   B. This testing is allowed of God
      1. For a purpose
      2. By design (it is exactly what is needed—customized)
   C. This testing is tailor-made
      1. As to weight
      2. As to length
   D. This testing is always associated with a way of escape
      1. An anomaly is involved—"a way to escape, that ye may be able to bear it"

2. There is a way out of temptation
3. There is a way through/over trials to escape the peril in them

E. The child of God can always be a winner

Conclusion:

It isn't a matter of a cliché or a "pious platitude"! This is a basic statement of fact. Our testings are in the human realm, and our God is faithful. He won't allow us to be overwhelmed, and He even promises a way out for us. You can't see it at all? You have either a wrong focus or a lack of faith.

How Are You Doing?

2 Corinthians 10:7–18

Introduction:

The title of the sermon is a set of words that are often said routinely and without meaning. But it is a valid question. Someone has said, "The self-examined life is the only life worth living," and, "An humble knowledge of thyself is a surer way to God than a deep search after leaning." Exactly how are you doing?

I. **Are You What You Claim to Be? (v. 10)**
    A. The charge against Paul
        1. Summarized in verse 10
            a. He writes a powerful letter
            b. When he comes, he won't back up his words
        2. The basic charge—there is a difference between his walk and his talk
    B. The real nature of that charge
        1. Paul wasn't what he claimed to be
        2. This charge frequently comes to Christians today
            a. Our walk and our talk don't match
            b. We appear "bigger than life" (in real life, no one is ever bigger than life)
    C. The way you can escape that charge
        1. Make sure you are what you claim to be
        2. Make sure that what you are is what you should be

II. **Are You Judging Yourself by a Valid Standard? (v. 12)**
    A. You can make yourself the standard
        1. It is somewhat correct—to measure yourself against what you have been
        2. But this quickly gets into some improper areas
            a. Self-righteous people make themselves the standard
            b. Christ addressed this teaching with the mote/beam story
    B. You can make other people the standard
        1. We have a strong tendency to compare ourselves to others
            a. So long as I am better than someone else
            b. So long as I am not as bad as someone else
        2. It is wrong to do so in many ways
            a. Others really don't matter

            b. You don't really know what others are or aren't
            c. You can find many others better than or not as
                bad as yourself
    C. You can judge yourself by God's standard
        1. We are to be like Christ
        2. We are to be like Christ would have us be
        3. We are driven to the Bible to determine what we
            are to be

III. **Are You Giving Credit to the One to Whom It Is Due?
      (v. 17)**
    A. Paul would give credit only to the Lord
        1. Throughout this section, Paul is crediting God
        2. Paul would not claim any authority not of God
    B. When you "glory," be sure it is in the Lord
        1. We all "glory" at times
            a. Sinful human nature makes us do it
            b. It is not necessarily bad
        2. The things in which we "glory"
            a. Personal appearance
            b. Personal accomplishments (those of our kids)
            c. Personal talents and abilities
            d. Personal property
            e. There is nothing that man possesses in which he
                is not prone to glory
    C. Why you should "glory" in the Lord (v. 18)
        1. The man who commends himself is not commended
        2. The only commendation that counts is that of the
            Lord

Conclusion:

   Christian living allows us to appreciate the ancient saying
attributed to the Buddha that to know oneself is the true; to
strive with oneself is the good; to conquer oneself is the beauti-
ful. How are you doing? Are you what you claim to be? Are you
judging yourself by God's standard? Are you giving the glory to
God for all you have and are? If your answer to any of these
questions is "no," then you are not doing well.

A Walk-Through Heart
2 Corinthians 7:2–16

Introduction:
There was a heart in a Chicago museum through which you could walk. It made the structure and function of the heart very plain. This chapter is a trip through the heart of Paul. Walk through it and see what's there.

I.   **The Propriety of Transparency (vv. 2–5)**
  A. We are trained never to let anyone into our hearts—"Don't admit anything," etc.
    1. It is not too hard for most of us to be that way
    2. It is questioned whether that approach is right, and Paul helps with an answer
  B. Understand the background
    1. He had written a letter—likely 1 Corinthians
    2. He had dealt firmly with many problems
    3. He had experienced second thoughts regarding it
  C. Paul reveals a tremendous amount of his inner self
    1. A clear conscience (v. 2)
    2. An unfeigned love (v. 3)
    3. Some contrasting emotions (vv. 4–5)
    4. A crushing concern—the outcome of his letter to them was much on his heart
    5. The need of affirmation
  D. This all speaks to issue of transparency
    1. It is obviously proper to do so
    2. Actually it is probably very positive to do so
  E. Paul was truly transparent in his heart

II. **The Essential of Encouragement (vv. 6–7, 13b–16)**
  A. All encouragement comes from God (v. 6)
    1. His character is such that He gives consolation to those who are anxious and depressed
    2. He uses various means to provide that comfort
  B. The means of encouragement
    1. The coming of Titus (v. 6)
    2. The message of Titus (v. 7)
      a. He brought word of their reaction to the letter
      b. He brought word of their continued love for Paul
    3. The experience of Titus (vv. 13b–16)
      a. He had been well received by the Corinthians
      b. His reception had confirmed all that Paul had said of them

C. Paul needed encouragement at this point, received it, and God used human means to communicate it

III. The Assurance of Understanding (vv. 8–11)
A. Paul's greatest fear? That the Corinthians would not understand
1. His reason for writing
2. His design in rebuking them
3. The end that he desired to see
B. It was obvious that they had understood at least these three things
1. They understood the role of reproof (v. 8) (Paul says, "I don't regret what I did in writing that letter—although I did for a while")
   a. A servant of God is required to reprove and rebuke
   b. There are six instructions in the Pastorals along this line (1 Tim. 5:1, 20; 2 Tim. 4:2; Titus 1:9, 13; 2:15)
2. They understood the reality of repentance (vv. 9–10)—Paul's reproof was designed to produce change in them
3. They understood the revelation of response (v. 11)
   a. This is a description of their reaction to his letter
   b. It records a genuine effort to make things right
   c. The strong words indicate the strength of their response
4. Paul was greatly relieved by the assurance that they understood what was really in his heart

IV. A Desired Relationship (vv. 12–13a)
A. Paul wanted a particular relationship with the Corinthians
1. He wanted something close
2. He wanted to care for them
3. He wanted them to care for him
B. His purpose in writing the letter comes in here
1. It wasn't just for the one who was sinning
2. It wasn't just for the one sinned against
3. It was for the relationship between them
C. Paul wanted a personal relationship rather than a professional one

Conclusion:
As you walk through Paul's heart, I trust that you can see his desire: He wanted to be transparent; he needed to be encouraged at times; he wanted others to understand why he did and said what he did; he wanted a mutually helpful relationship; he wanted to be lovers—two hearts that beat as one.

Inner Renewal

2 Corinthians 4:13–18

Introduction:

Bold statements are most meaningful when backed by bold action! Paul makes a bold statement here that is backed by action. He has already said that we have the treasure of spiritual reality in earthen vessels of humanity so that credit for accomplishment will go to God rather than to us. As a result, trouble is a normal part of the Christian life. How shall we then handle it?

I.   **Resolution—"We faint not!" (v. 16a)**
   A.   A repeat of the opening statement in the chapter
   B.   Meaning "we don't lose heart, turn aside, quit"
      1.   We may feel weak
      2.   We may sometimes want to quit

II.   **Reasons (vv. 13–15)—"For which cause" (v. 16a)**
   A.   We are sure of ultimate triumph (vv. 13–14)
      1.   Note Psalm 116—a psalm of triumph
      2.   It states the certainty of the resurrection
   B.   We are sure we benefit others (v. 15a)
      1.   All that is being endured has an effect on others
      2.   By his example of faithfulness even in suffering, Paul was influencing others to do likewise
   C.   We are sure God is being glorified (v. 15b)
      1.   Handling the sufferings brought glory to the Lord
      2.   Endurance was an answer to the prayers of many thus also glorifying the Lord

III.   **Reality (v. 16b)**
   A.   The outward person is perishing
      1.   Outward man—all that is visible (more than just physical)
      2.   Is perishing—continuative sense—going steadily downhill
      3.   This was the result of natural and supernatural problems
   B.   The inner person is renewed day by day
      1.   Inner person—that which is invisible (spiritual)
      2.   Is being renewed—continuative sense—receiving fresh impartation
      3.   Result of something special happening

IV. Resources—How are we being renewed daily?
  A. It is the work of the Holy Spirit
    1. His inner witness and ministry
    2. It is almost always in connection with the Word of God
  B. The efficacy of prayer
    1. The promise that we are being heard
    2. The assurance from experience that He answers
  C. Knowledge born of experience
    1. We know certain things from the experience of walking with Him
    2. The longer we walk with Him, the less we are affected by outward things
  D. The fellowship of the saints
    1. We gain great encouragement from the support of others
    2. We gain great encouragement from the experience of others

V. Recognition (vv. 17–18)
  A. A proper evaluation—our affliction
    1. Is characterized as
       a. Light in comparison
       b. But for a moment in the actual scope of things
    2. Will result in an eternal weight of glory
       a. Limited to things suffered in connection with faith
       b. See James 1:12
  B. A proper focus
    1. "We look at"—"to fix one's gaze, to concentrate one's attention upon"
    2. The contrast
       a. We look not at things that are seen—outward
       b. We look at things that are not seen—inner
    3. The reason
       a. The outward is not real, but the unseen is real
       b. This is the absolute opposite of normal thinking

Conclusion:

The outward person is perishing, but we faint not because we have inner resources sufficient to keep us going until we see Him. The needed secret is to keep your perspective and concentrate your focus. We can say, "We faint not!" We can back our brave statement with courageous actions.

Earthen Vessels

2 Corinthians 4:7–12

Introduction:
Progress in the Lord's work is often very difficult. Our personal spiritual progress is also very hard and time-consuming. We often wonder why. There is some measure of explanation here in this passage.

I. **A Paradox—"But we have this treasure in earthen vessels" (v. 7a)**
    A. The nature of a paradox—an apparently contradictory statement that is actually true
    B. The particular paradox here
        1. The treasure—the gospel, the Christian faith, ministry, etc.
        2. Earthen vessels—pots made of clay and the plainest possible
    C. The treasure of the Good News from God is entrusted to the commonest, most flawed vessels

II. **Its Purpose—"That the excellency of the power may be of God, and not of us" (v. 7b)**
    A. This has been done purposely and for reason
    B. The reason is so that
        1. It will be obvious that any success is traceable to God
        2. It will be obvious that any power is from God
    C. A better modern likeness might be battered tools in a wood shop
        1. It is obvious that the skill does not lie in the tools
        2. It draws attention to the artisan

III. **Some Illustrations**
    A. "We are troubled on every side, yet not distressed" (v. 8a)
        1. The hiker on a trail that leads to an ever narrowing canyon
        2. No matter how narrow though, there is still room to maneuver
    B. "We are perplexed, but not in despair" (v. 8b)
        1. The traveler faced with various choices, most of which appear bad
        2. We are never brought to total loss (confused but not confounded)

C. "[We are] persecuted, but not forsaken" (v. 9a)
   1. The quarry—animals being hunted
   2. We are never actually captured (even martyrdom is escape)
D. "[We are] cast down, but not destroyed" (v. 9b)
   1. The wrestler who is often thrown for a fall
   2. We are never pinned for the count

We have a great treasure. It is entrusted to common vessels. We are continually reminded of this by things that happen, *but* His power is committed to us, and that is obvious because we are never quite knocked out. Thus, we survive, and the credit goes to Him

IV. **A Promise—"Always bearing about in the body the dying of the Lord Jesus, that the life also of Jesus might be made manifest in our body" (v. 10)**
   A. This is a statement of fact
      1. We bear the same kinds of sufferings that led to His death
      2. This goes on all the time
   B. The reason
      1. So our continuing to live will show His life in us
      2. We are living illustrations of His resurrection
      3. Verse 11 is a further explanation of this truth

V. **A Summary—"So then death worketh in us, but life in you" (v. 12)**
   A. Paul says that it is tough for him and the other apostles
      1. "Death worketh in us"—we experience things that could lead to death
      2. This is going on all the time
   B. But there is a good result
      1. You are benefited by what we suffer
      2. You get to see what God can do

Conclusion:

This passage provides
   - Explanation—The reason for the difficulty? That we might be constantly reminded of our inadequacy and His sufficiency.
   - Encouragement—We should not be discouraged by the difficulties as they are just part of the normal course of life.
   - Enablement—The difficulties provide the vehicle through which He can manifest His power.
   - Endorsement—The difficulties are an indication that a person or ministry is authentic.

Give Yourself the Best Present

2 Corinthians 2:5–11

Introduction:

The importance of forgiveness cannot be over stressed. If you have ever given yourself a gift, here is a suggestion for the next one. What is the best gift you could give yourself? How about this one?

I. **The Phases of Forgiveness**
    A. Forgive from the heart (Matt. 18:35; Mark 11:25)
        1. It can be done immediately
        2. It does not depend in any way on what the other person does
        3. It is a commandment, not an option
    B. Grant forgiveness (Luke 17:3–4)
        1. It can only be done "on request"
        2. It is easy once you forgive from the heart
        3. This forgiveness must be unconditional
    C. Restoration
        1. The question in church—can one be restored?
            a. The process is repentance, recognition, admission, sorrow, turning
            b. Once the fruits of repentance have been demonstrated, restoration is possible
        2. The parallel in personal life
            a. There must be repentance
            b. It may take time to rebuild relationship
        3. It is an area in which to tread lightly

II. **The Freedom of Forgiveness**
    A. Frees from bitterness
        1. Bitterness is the culmination of a process
        2. Unforgiveness leads to bitterness
        3. Bitterness "defiles" others
    B. Frees from grieving the Holy Spirit
        1. Bitterness is a cause of grief to Him
        2. Grieving the Holy Spirit is a dangerous game
    C. Frees from domination by the past
        1. Offenses are always "past tense" matters
        2. Forgiveness places them in the past and gets one's focus off them

D. Frees from someone else's determining one's spirit
    1. An unforgiving spirit keeps one in bondage to the one unforgiven
    2. Forgiveness allows one to determine the course of one's life
E. Frees from sitting in judgment on everyone else
    1. Judgment is not my responsibility
    2. Failure to forgive involves me in what I was never intended to do
    3. There is extra stress when I do what I am not supposed to do

III. **The Failure of Forgiveness**
    A. It disobeys specific commandments
        1. Disobedience is disobedience
        2. The Bible is very clear on this subject
    B. It shows me as the hypocrite I really am
        1. I refuse to give what I have been given
        2. We look for hypocrisy in the wrong places (Matt. 18:23–25)
    C. It rejects Christlikeness
        1. We are to be like Christ
        2. Christ epitomizes forgiveness (Luke 23:34)
    D. It jeopardizes answered prayer
        1. We come to God on a basis we don't offer another person
        2. Unforgiveness may explain unanswered prayer
    E. It runs the risk of bitterness
        1. A forgiving person is never a bitter person
        2. Bitterness is one of the most destructive of human emotions
    F. It risks loss of forgiveness
        1. This is a very difficult passage to interpret
        2. It appears to teach that unwillingness to forgive others may affect our ability to find forgiveness
    G. It gives Satan an advantage
        1. Paul was concerned about that in Corinth
        2. It allows him an area in which to do his work
    H. It provides a negative example
        1. There are always those who watch us
        2. This is especially true of children
    I. It hinders the work of God's church
        1. Strife within can hinder spiritual progress
        2. Strife can become contagious (we seldom completely keep our bitterness to ourselves)

J. It destroys testimony
1. An unforgiving Christian is an anomaly
2. It likely will not go undetected by the unconverted world

Conclusion:

This teaching sounds strange and incorrect, but the best gift you can give yourself is to forgive others. You have everything to gain and nothing to lose! Will you give yourself that best possible gift?

Here's That Woman Again
John 4:16–24

Introduction:

Here's that woman at the well again. There is much current emphasis on worship, and it appears that most people don't know much about it. This is the reason some seldom speak of a worship service; many worship services really aren't. Possibly we can learn some things from this passage about the subject.

I.   **The Superiority of Scripture in Worship (v. 22)**
    A.   "Ye worship ye know not what"
        1.   Notice "what" rather than "whom"
        2.   This refers to their whole system and condemns it with ignorance
    B.   "For salvation is of the Jews"
        1.   An obvious contrast intended here
        2.   "You don't know what you are after, but the Jews have it"
    C.   The difference here
        1.   It is obviously not one of racial prejudice (vv. 4, 9)
        2.   The Samaritans refused all of Scripture but the Pentateuch
            a.   They thus were impoverished of much of God's revelation
            b.   The Jewish system took account of all of Scripture and, thus, gave them better knowledge of who and what they worshiped
    D.   The worship of the Jews was based on knowledge—an indispensable part of true worship!

II.   **The Significance of the Spiritual in Worship (v. 24)**
    A.   "God is spirit"
        1.   Original does not include *a*
        2.   This deals with the essential nature of God
    B.   "They that worship him must worship him in spirit"
        1.   If we are to worship God, it must be on the basis of His nature
        2.   Our worship must be of the spirit (human spirit in view)
    C.   True worship must be internal to be meaningful
        1.   Worship is never accomplished in that which is merely outward

      2. To have meaning, externals in worship must come from the heart

      3. The outward has its place, but it is never of primary importance

   D. Spiritual worship is not an option—"must"—worship is really not an individual matter—it is not up to the individual!

III. The Symmetry of the Stresses in Worship

   A. ". . . worship in spirit and truth"

      1. Second *in* is not in the original—spirit and truth are linked

      2. Two aspects of worship are in view

         a. Spirit—internal, emotional, experiential

         b. Truth—revelational, logical, rational, cognitive

      3. Both are necessary

   B. Balance is necessary

      1. Worship must be founded in and bounded by the Word of God

      2. Worship must be energized by and expressed with the spirit

   C. Balance will produce

      1. Spoken truth

      2. Sincerity of spirit

      3. Acted truth (to speak of worship while actively disobeying the Word of God is hypocrisy)

Conclusion:

A good deal of what passes for worship today is nothing of the kind! Worship must be an internal expression that accords with truth (both believed and acted). We face a danger in worship; we are often so much on the truth side that we miss the spirit side. Feelings must be bounded by the Word, but there is a place for them in worship. How are you worshiping the Lord in your life? Is your worship marked by both spirit and truth?

The Heart of Passionate Christianity

Genesis 22:1–14

Introduction:
"If it is supposed to be cold, make it cold. If it is supposed to be hot, make it hot!" This is not only the cry of a true gourmand, it is also—according to Scripture—the cry of God in regard to His people.

I.   **The Priority of Passion—An all-surpassing love**
    A.   The pain of Abraham
        1.   His priceless possession—his son
        2.   His peculiar possession—his only son
        3.   His precious possession—his only son that he loved
        4.   His paternal possession—he was the father to that son
    B.   The plan for Abraham
        1.   A painful sacrifice
        2.   A personal sacrifice
        3.   A premeditated sacrifice
    C.   The purpose for Abraham—to test his love
    D.   The practical issue involved—the danger of idolatry in the life of Abraham

II.   **The Policy of Passion—An unquestioning obedience**
    A.   The request to Abraham
        1.   It was perplexing (he would say, "I don't get it!")
        2.   It was actually prohibited (he would say, "I can't do it")
    B.   The response of Abraham
        1.   It was prompt (v. 3a)
        2.   It was prepared (v. 3b)
        3.   It was personal (v. 5a)
        4.   It was praise-filled (5b)
        5.   It was precise (v. 9)
        6.   It was pure (v. 10)
    C.   The practical issue involved—"Would Abraham obey or show insubordination?"

III.   **The Principle of Passion—An unwavering faith**
    A.   There are five separate statements that
        1.   Reveal the results of his faith (vv. 1, 11)
           a.   True faith follows and finishes
           b.   Weak faith forsakes and falters

2. Reveal the reality of his faith (v. 5)
    a. Note the personal pronoun here
    b. There is an expanded explanation in Hebrews 11:17–19 that is necessary to understanding the complete picture
3. Reveal the reason for his faith (vv. 8, 14)
    a. He looked to "Jehovah-Jireh"—the Lord will provide
    b. Abraham had absolute confidence in God's ability
B. The practical issue involved—to test the confidence of Abraham

Conclusion:

This must have been an incredible experience for Abraham, but it put his faith to the test and created a genuine spiritual passion within him. Although they are lesser tests, God puts us to the test for the same purposes as He tested Abraham.

Our Battle with Sin

Psalm 51

Introduction:

Most people wage a constant war with sin, far too often losing the individual battles. God has made provision for our warfare and shown us many important things about the enemy we face.

I. **The Definition of Sin**
    A. "Transgressions" (v. 1)—stepping over the line
    B. "Iniquity" (v. 2)—twisting or perverting
    C. "Sin" (v. 3)—falling short of the mark
    D. "Evil" (v. 4)—completely rotten or vile

II. **The Devastation of Sin**
    A. It affects your sight (v. 3)
    B. It affects your hearing (v. 8)
    C. It affects your speech (vv. 13, 15)—there is no witness and no praise
    D. It affects your whole body (v. 3)—there is a complete internal collapse (Ps. 32:3–4)
    E. It affects your mind (v. 6)—internal deceit leaves one where one can't think straight
    F. It affects your spirit (v. 10)
    G. It affects your heart (v. 10)

III. **The Defeat of Sin**
    A. It is an intellectual issue (v. 3)
    B. It is a personal issue
    C. It is a verbal issue—"confession"—to say the same thing as God
    D. It is a theological issue
        1. Sin is always against God
        2. Sin is always forgivable
    E. It is a logical issue
    F. It is an internal issue (vv. 16–17)

Conclusion:

It is not necessary for us to allow sin to have dominion over us. He has already defeated it; we must appropriate His victory and make it practical on a daily basis.

"Out of Control?"

Galatians 5:22–23

Introduction:
A definition of self-control—literally, to grab, hold, strength, mastery. It becomes "the ability to restrain passions and appetites." It particularly involves paying a price (1 Cor. 9:24–27). Here are seven steps to self-control.

I. **Admit Your Problem**
 A. Our instinct is to excuse ourselves and shift blame
 B. The key concept—individual, personal responsibility

II. **An Attitude of Faith**
 A. We already have the power to transform our lives (Rom. 12:2)
 B. We have a protection from defeat already provided (1 Cor. 10:13)

III. **Address the Past**
 A. A focus on past failures almost assures a repeat performance
 B. We can't change the past; we should stop trying to do so!

IV. **Argue with Feelings**
 A. Learn to say *no* to yourself (Titus 2:11–14)
 B. Much failure of self-control is simply a failure to resist urges, etc.

V. **An Accountability to Change**
 A. Never underestimate the power of partnership (Eccl. 4:12)
 B. This separates the whiners from the winners

VI. **Avoid Danger Spots**
 A. Don't keep falling into the same ditch
 B. Analyze people, places, times, things

VII. **Appeal to God for Help**
 A. Maintain constant communication with God (Heb. 2:18; 4:15–16)
 B. Maintain a powerful preoccupation with God (Matt. 22:37)

Conclusion:
Self-control has applications in at least five areas: physical discipline, mental discipline, moral discipline, devotional discipline, and social discipline.

The Power of Gentleness

Galatians 5:22–23

Introduction:

In the "dog eat dog" society with which we are all so familiar, the very sound of the word *gentleness* seems out of place. But one of the aspects of the fruit of the Spirit is that very thing, gentleness!

I. **The Problem of Gentleness**
   A. The word is used interchangeably with meekness and humility
   B. The idea is usually associated with weakness, passivity, and compromise
   C. Its true meaning, however, is that of power under control and strength balanced with tenderness

II. **The Patterns of Gentleness**
   A. The Old Testament pattern—Moses (Num. 12:3)
      1. He was a man of passion and compassion (Exod. 32:19, 32)
      2. That combination rendered him a great leader
   B. The New Testament pattern—Christ (2 Cor. 10:1)
      1. He was a model of righteous indignation (Matt. 16:33; 21:12–14; Mark 3:1–6)
      2. Christ indicates that gentleness includes the power to be properly angry

III. **The Profile of Gentleness—What will gentleness look like?**
   A. In our relationship to God (James 1:21)
      1. Willingness to submit
      2. This submission ought to be particularly directed toward His Word
   B. In our routines of life (1 Peter 3:4)
      1. It will make us understanding rather than demanding
      2. It will make us willing to admit wrong
      3. It will make us willing to listen to others
   C. In our responsibility to confront wrong (Gal. 6:1)
      1. It will make us gracious and not judgmental
      2. It will make correction a stimulant rather than a depressant

D. In our response to disagreement and even mistreatment (2 Tim. 2:15)
  1. Our extreme tendencies are to either react or retreat
  2. We are to be actors rather than reactors
E. In our respect for unbelievers (1 Peter 3:12)
  1. We should show acceptance and love
  2. It's an old cliché, but . . . we must love the sinner even though we hate the sin

Conclusion:

We use the term *gentleman* rather loosely. It ought to be that every Christian is characterized by gentleness so that *gentleman* or *gentlewoman* is an apt description of him or her.

Somewhere in Between
Revelation 3:14–19

Introduction:
Jesus makes very clear His distaste for anything lukewarm. It appears He would rather have His people cold spiritually than hanging in between cold and hot.

I.   **Its Characteristics**
    A. It is not open rebellion
    B. Its is much more indifference
        1. It lacks commitment
        2. It lacks involvement
        3. It lacks excitement
        4. It lacks challenge

II. **Its Causes—It involves a series of failures**
    A. Failure to understand the truth
    B. Failure to practice obedience
    C. Failure to apply Scriptures
    D. Failure to express gratitude (especially to God)
    E. Failure to make a mental commitment
    F. Failure to make regular progress

III. **Its Curse**
    A. It is an irritant to the Lord
    B. It threatens judgment
    C. It causes us to be rootless
    D. It robs of joy
    E. It destroys testimony

IV. **Its Cure**
    A. A decision of the mind and will
    B. A direction of the heart
    C. A dedication of the spirit

Conclusion:
In a day when people appear to have trouble making up their minds about most anything spiritual, God warns us about being "cool" Christians and calls upon us to be "on fire" for Him.